"I told Phil that I wasn't interested. It seems a daft idea to me,
writing a book about an ordinary guitar that I bought at Manny's"
David Gilmour

PINK FLOYD THE BLACK STRAT

A HISTORY OF DAVID GILMOUR'S BLACK FENDER STRATOCASTER©

PHIL TAYLOR

HAL LEONARD BOOKS

NEW YORK

Second edition, updated and expanded

Published in 2008 by Hal Leonard Books
An Imprint of Hal Leonard Corporation
7777 West Bluemound Road
Milwaukee, WI 53213

Trade Book Division Editorial Offices
19 West 21st Street, New York, NY 10010

First edition published in Great Britain in 2007
by theblackstrat.com

Printed in the United States of America

Library of Congress Cataloging-in-
Publication Data is available upon request.

ISBN 978-1-4234-4559-3

www.halleonard.com

Half title: Relaxing at David's with Blackie the cat
Title page: 'The Wave' North Coyote Buttes, Paria
Canyon/Vermillion Cliffs Wilderness, Arizona, USA

INTRO

In May 1970 Pink Floyd guitarist David Gilmour flew via New York on his return to London. He needed to buy a new Fender Stratocaster. The band had been forced to end their US tour early due to the theft of their equipment in New Orleans. Although most of it was recovered, their guitars were not.

And so begins the story of one of the most famous guitars in the history of rock music – David Gilmour's Black Strat. Purchased as a standard model Fender Stratocaster off the shop floor in Manny's Music, New York, the music created with this humble Strat has entered into the homes and lives of quite literally billions of people. Through live broadcasts, radio play, album sales, film and television appearances, this iconic guitar has appeared at most Pink Floyd concerts and on every Pink Floyd album from 1970 to 1983. It can be heard on David's solo projects in 1978, 1984, and again in 2006. The Black Strat has travelled the world over and David has played it with other artists including Paul McCartney, Kate Bush and Roy Harper.

This book explores the history of his Black Stratocaster, from its early days as David's primary guitar in Pink Floyd to its fall from favour, subsequent resurrection at the 2005 Live8 Pink Floyd reunion and return to being his Stratocaster of choice.

Since 1974 I have had the pleasure of being the custodian of the Black Strat. It has been through numerous modifications, had a variety of necks, pick-ups and bridges. I have cared for, handled, dismantled, modified, adjusted, restrung, polished, tuned, plugged in, tested and handed it over to David on countless occasions throughout the years. I have also packed it away safely, transported it to and from his home, airports, live venues, recording studios, television studios, warehouses, rehearsal rooms, taken it for repair and generally seen to its maintenance and safe keeping for over three decades.

This is my account of the Black Strat, drawn from my memories, the historical documentation and David's recollections. Where our memories have faltered, much research has been undertaken in order to ascertain the correct factual content.

Phil Taylor

1 **BEFORE THE BLACK**

DAVID GILMOUR'S ELECTRIC GUITARS 1968/70
THE WHITE TELECASTER

The history of 'The Black Strat' must inevitably begin with a brief look at David's first Fender Telecaster and Stratocaster guitars.

In March 1967, David's parents bought him his first Fender guitar, a white Telecaster with a rosewood neck and white pickguard. It was purchased as his 21st birthday present in New York where his parents were living at the time.

David was asked to join Pink Floyd (then Syd Barrett, Nick Mason, Roger Waters and Rick Wright) on the 6th January 1968, as the second guitar player and vocalist. Syd Barrett's departure from the band was officially announced on the 6th April 1968, although his participation ended much earlier. David began playing with Pink Floyd using the Telecaster, with one of Syd's Teles as his spare.

Syd turned up unexpectedly at Abbey Road Studios during one of the recording sessions for *A Saucerful Of Secrets* and repossessed his guitar. David was left with only one guitar, his Telecaster, but this association was to be short-lived. In July 1968, Pink Floyd flew to America for their second US tour. During this trip the airline lost his guitar, it has never been recovered.

Facing page: At Abbey Road Studios recording 'A Saucerful Of Secrets'
Below: At Abbey Road Studio 2 with June Child
Right: Performing at The Paradiso, Amsterdam, May 1968

THE FIRST WHITE STRATOCASTER

David had always wanted a 'Hank Marvin' guitar. Marvin, an early influence, was the guitarist with 'The Shadows' and the first musician in England to have a Stratocaster.

When David first joined Pink Floyd he had only one guitar, his white Telecaster, so the band bought him a new Strat. This late sixties model was white with a rosewood neck and a white pickguard. It became his main guitar with the white Telecaster carried as his spare (prior to its loss by the airline).

Right: Hank B. Marvin
Below: West Berlin, March 1970
Below right: David and Roy Harper at the Hyde Park free concert, June 1968

The day before *A Saucerful Of Secrets* was released, he played the new Strat at the Hyde Park free concert in London on the 28th June 1968, then in the Netherlands, and on the 1968 US tour. After the loss of his first Telecaster, David acquired a Tele with a natural brown wood finish, a maple neck and a white pickguard. He now carried this as his spare (later used for some Atom Heart Mother shows). The white Strat was used for live performances throughout 1969 and into the early part of 1970, and for recording *More*, *Ummagumma* and *Zabriskie Point*.

Pink Floyd with Frank Zappa playing David's brown Telecaster at The Actuel Pop and Jazz Festival at Mont de l'Enclus in Amougies, Belgium, October 1969

THE FIRST BLACK STRATOCASTER

Below centre: A black Fender Stratocaster with rosewood neck (replica of stolen 1969 model)
Below right (top): Clip from KQED TV Show, San Fransisco, April 1970
Below right (bottom): Pink Floyd with their equipment

On 9th April 1970 Pink Floyd set off on their third tour of the US, taking their custom built Azimuth co-ordinator multi-speaker pan pot system that enabled them to perform concerts with quadraphonic sound.

The tour began at the sold-out Fillmore East in New York. David did not take his Telecaster on this tour as he was planning to buy a second Strat at Manny's Music (the renowned musical instrument store on West 48th in Manhattan). There he purchased a black Strat with a rosewood neck and a white pickguard for use as a spare or alternative to his white Strat.

Towards the end of the US tour, disaster struck when all of the band's equipment was stolen. The theft occurredon the 16th May 1970 during concert dates at The Warehouse, New Orleans. Pink Floyd's hired truck containing all of their equipment was taken. Inside the truck were two electric guitars, two bass guitars, an electronic organ, two drum kits, a 4,000 watt PA system with twelve speaker cabinets, five Binson echo units, microphones and ten miles of cable. Fortunately, most of the equipment was recovered.

On hearing of their plight, a receptionist at the band's hotel contacted her father who was in the FBI. They managed to find the missing truck along with all of the equipment - except the guitars. Both David's white Strat and his new black Strat, as well as Roger's two bass guitars, were never seen again. The few remaining dates of the US tour were cancelled.

David flew home to London via New York, returning to Manny's Music only six weeks after his last purchase. As a replacement for the stolen guitars, he bought his second black Stratocaster, his first with a maple neck. It marked the rather ordinary begin-ning of the extraordinary life of 'The Black Strat', the now famous guitar and subject of this book.

Above: Recording at Capitol Studios, Hollywood May 1970
Below: A black Fender Stratocaster with maple neck circa 1969

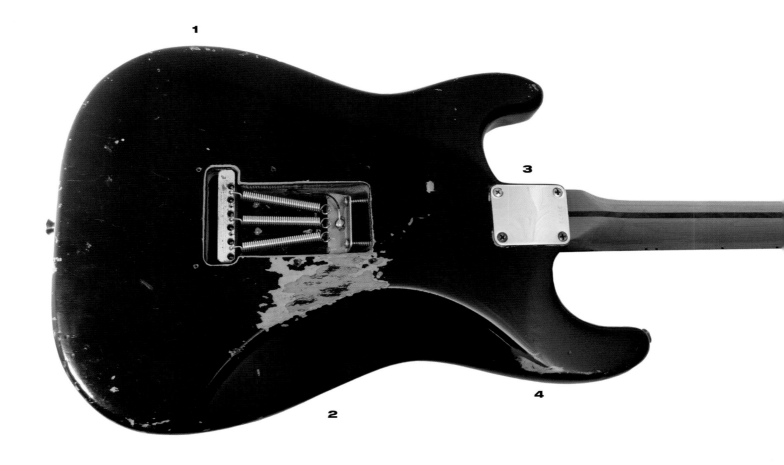

2 THE BLACK

ORIGINAL SPECIFICATIONS OF THE BLACK STRAT, MAY 1970

Above and facing page:
The Black Strat with current
1983 neck and black pickguard

A standard black Fender Stratocaster CBS-era model, it had a white pickguard, a maple neck with a 'maple cap' fingerboard and a large headstock. There are no original dates to be found anywhere on the guitar. Opinions vary on the dates that Fender made changes, but it appears to have been built with parts from both 1968 and 1969 (the current neck is not original and the later pot date codes are from 1971). The guitar was, in all probability, constructed in 1969 and then purchased in May 1970 by David from Manny's Music.

THE BODY

1 The black paint on the body predates the change made by Fender in 1968 when they started using two coats of Alphatic Urethane (UAC), also known as polycoating. They had previously used multiple coats of clearcoat lacquer

2 The contour of the Alder wood body was used by Fender from 1966 through the late 60's

3 The original serial number 266936 (see illustration on page 17) is from the 1969 period. Fender used serial numbers in the 250000 to 280000 range during 1969

4 The worn paintwork reveals red with yellow underneath – originally sprayed sunburst then oversprayed black as a custom colour

5 The routing of the body cavity for the pickups is pre-1970. (Fender routing is more 'rounded' on the corners before 1970)

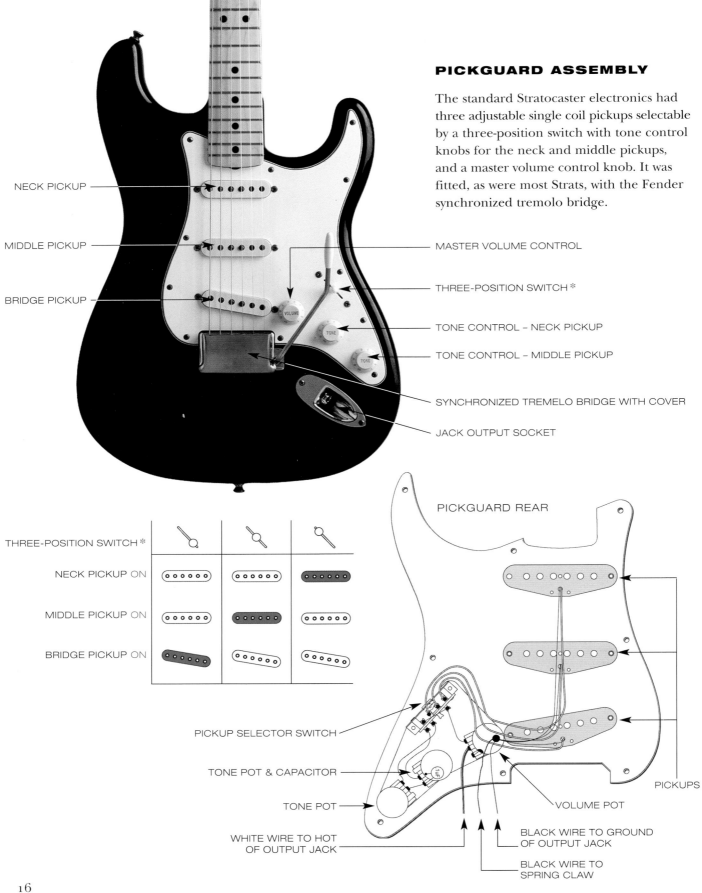

PICKGUARD ASSEMBLY

The standard Stratocaster electronics had three adjustable single coil pickups selectable by a three-position switch with tone control knobs for the neck and middle pickups, and a master volume control knob. It was fitted, as were most Strats, with the Fender synchronized tremolo bridge.

NECK PICKUP

MIDDLE PICKUP

BRIDGE PICKUP

MASTER VOLUME CONTROL

THREE-POSITION SWITCH *

TONE CONTROL – NECK PICKUP

TONE CONTROL – MIDDLE PICKUP

SYNCHRONIZED TREMELO BRIDGE WITH COVER

JACK OUTPUT SOCKET

THREE-POSITION SWITCH *

NECK PICKUP ON

MIDDLE PICKUP ON

BRIDGE PICKUP ON

PICKGUARD REAR

PICKUP SELECTOR SWITCH

TONE POT & CAPACITOR

TONE POT

WHITE WIRE TO HOT
OF OUTPUT JACK

VOLUME POT

PICKUPS

BLACK WIRE TO GROUND
OF OUTPUT JACK

BLACK WIRE TO
SPRING CLAW

16

THE NECK

1 The original neck had a late sixties-type enlarged peghead, first introduced in 1965, with a thick black Fender logo on it. This type of logo was first used by Fender in 1968

2 The neck plate was a four-bolt plate with a large 'F' beneath the serial number (four-bolt neck plates were used by Fender from 1950 to mid 1971). The 'F' appeared in 1965

3 The tuners were chrome plated with a large 'F' stamped on the back cover. (These 'F' tuners were used by Fender on Strats from late 1967)

4 The original neck with a 'maple cap' fingerboard was uncommon in 1969 – rosewood was typically used. There was no 'skunk stripe' on the rear as the truss rod was inserted from the front

5 The current neck is a one piece maple neck with a walnut 'skunk stripe' down the back where the truss rod was installed. Fender used these from 1950-1959 and then from 1970 onwards

6 It is fitted with Gotoh 'Kluson style' tuners

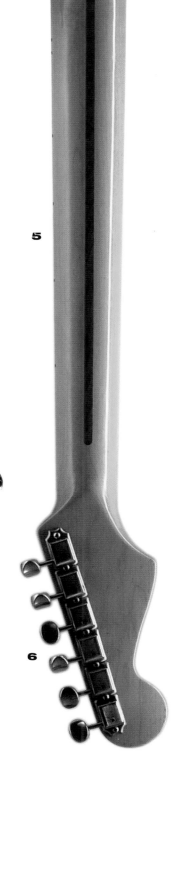

DEBUT APPEARANCE OF THE BLACK STRAT, JUNE 1970

When David purchased the Black Strat, Pink Floyd were in the process of recording a new album. This record, later released as *Atom Heart Mother*, broke new ground as it featured a single twenty-five minute piece that stretched over an entire side of the album. It also included session musicians, and showcased a choir and a brass section for the first time on a Pink Floyd album.

The band began recording *Atom Heart Mother* in March 1970, taking a break to tour the US in April and May. During these sessions, David used his white Strat. When the band returned to recording the album in June, he used a sunburst Strat he had been given along with his newly purcahased Black Strat. This marked the first time it was used on a Pink Floyd record.

David's first live performance using the Black Strat was at the now legendary Festival of Blues and Progressive Music at Bath Showground near Shepton Mallet, England. This huge, two-day event on the 27th–28th June 1970 was a fitting debut for the guitar and featured the top bands of the time. It attracted twice the anticipated audience (approximately 150,000 people) and the congestion generated by the festival caused the biggest traffic jams in Somerset's history.

Pink Floyd's set included *A Saucerful Of Secrets, Set The Controls For The Heart Of The Sun* and a new piece introduced as *The Amazing Pudding*, later renamed *Atom Heart Mother*. DISC & MUSIC ECHO reported:

> "We were into the early hours of Sunday morning before Pink Floyd made it on stage. They took a very long time to set up, but their act was worth it. People were getting tired but the spectacular close to their set woke everyone up. After laying down some good sounds, they were joined by a choir about twelve-strong, and a brass section, and went into a twenty-minute thing which will be one side of their new album. It was a heavenly sound with a fireworks display that lit up the heavens. The finale saw three flares bursting open the sky with a galaxy of colours – smoke and the light show flooded the stage. It was amazing."

The next day Pink Floyd played at the Kralingen Pop Festival in Rotterdam, The Netherlands. David appeared on stage playing the Black Strat. The festival was filmed and excerpts were released on video as *Stamping Ground*.

Previous page: Aerial view of Bath Showground during Bath Festival of Blues and Progressive Music, June 1970 Below: Bath Festival programme

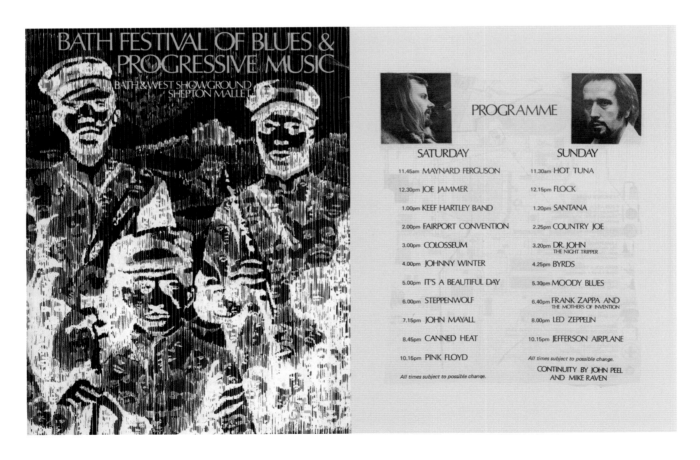

BATH FESTIVAL OF BLUES & PROGRESSIVE MUSIC

BATH & WEST SHOWGROUND SHEPTON MALLET

PROGRAMME

SATURDAY	SUNDAY
11.45am MAYNARD FERGUSON	11.30am HOT TUNA
12.30pm JOE JAMMER	12.15pm FLOCK
1.00pm KEEF HARTLEY BAND	1.20pm SANTANA
2.00pm FAIRPORT CONVENTION	2.25pm COUNTRY JOE
3.00pm COLOSSEUM	3.20pm DR. JOHN THE NIGHT TRIPPER
4.00pm JOHNNY WINTER	4.25pm BYRDS
5.00pm IT'S A BEAUTIFUL DAY	5.30pm MOODY BLUES
6.00pm STEPPENWOLF	6.40pm FRANK ZAPPA AND THE MOTHERS OF INVENTION
7.15pm JOHN MAYALL	8.00pm LED ZEPPELIN
8.45pm CANNED HEAT	10.15pm JEFFERSON AIRPLANE
10.15pm PINK FLOYD	*All times subject to possible change.*
All times subject to possible change.	CONTINUITY BY JOHN PEEL AND MIKE RAVEN

On stage, Kralingen Pop Festival, June 1970

HOLLAND **POP** FESTIVAL 70

SOFT MACHINE
BYRDS PINK FLOYD
JEFFERSON AIRPLANE

en vele andere topgroepen
op 26, 27 en 28 juni   in het

KRALINGSE BOS ROTTERDAM

3 BETWEEN THE BLACK

SUNBURST STRATOCASTER
JULY 1970

David was not completely satisfied with his new Black Strat and over the next few months he experimented with a variety of other guitars.

At the Blackhill Enterprises Free concert in Hyde Park, London on 18th July, Pink Floyd played *Atom Heart Mother,* as the new piece was now called, with a choir and brass section. David used a sunburst Strat with a rosewood neck and a white pickguard. This guitar had been given to him by Steve Marriott of Humble Pie/Small Faces fame. It was made from two different guitars – a 1963 rosewood neck with a 1959 body. Although he didn't use it for very long, David liked the neck on the guitar and would later swap it with the neck on the Black Strat. On occasions he then carried this sunburst as his spare guitar, fitted with the maple neck.

Right: Hyde Park Free Concert July 1970 Storm Thorgerson is standing on the left with camera at the ready

SECOND WHITE STRATOCASTER
AUGUST 1970

Pink Floyd played in France at the Saint Tropez Music Festival on 8th August 1970. The show was filmed and later broadcast by French TV. For this performance, David used a white Strat with a rosewood neck. This, his second white Strat (the first having been stolen in New Orleans the previous May) had been pur-

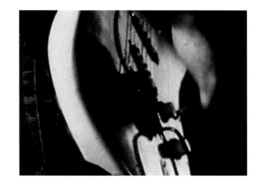

Above: The white Fender Stratocaster as it is today Inset: Clip from a French TV film of the Saint Tropez Music Festival 1970 shows David playing the white Stratocaster

chased second hand in England and had been poorly hand-painted in white over an already white finish. David removed the pickup covers, one of the first of many modifications to his guitars. In the early seventies while living in his flat on Old Brompton Road, London, he stripped the body of it's white paint to expose the natural wood finish. It now has custom stereo pickups, which were fitted in 1976.

NATURAL BROWN TELECASTER
SEPTEMBER 1970

Pink Floyd performed at the Fête de l'Humanité, Grand Scène, Bois de Vincennes, Paris, on 12th September, to over 500,000 people – their largest single concert attendance. At this show, David played his natural brown Telecaster with a maple neck. The performance was recorded by French TV (but never broadcast) and included *Atom Heart Mother*, complete with a choir and brass section. David had been carrying this guitar as his spare and it was used by Frank Zappa when he played with Pink Floyd at the Amougies Festival in September 1969. Occasionally David would use this Tele for performances of Atom Heart Mother through 1971. It appears on the back of the *Ummagumma* album – the only guitar featured on the cover that wasn't stolen during the previous US tour.

Right: Paris, September 1970
Below: Lyon, June 1971

David playing the Gibson Les Paul TV

LES PAUL TV, OCTOBER 1970

After the performance in Paris, Pink Floyd headed to North America for their fourth tour of the US. Referred to as the Atom Heart Mother World Tour (the *Atom Heart Mother* album was released on 10th October), it began at The Electric Factory in Philadelphia on 26th September and lasted until the end of October. THE SABOT in Seattle reported:

> "They produced a sound that at once give me fantasies of outer space. At times, the guitarist was seated with his back almost directly to the audience, doing things to his instrument in a manner reminiscent of the ape with the bone in *2001* (the film), and playing his own instrument panel on his amps."

Whilst in Seattle for performances, David visited a local pawn shop and purchased two guitars: one being a fifties Fender double neck pedal steel guitar – later to be used for slide on *One Of These Days* from *Meddle* and then on *The Dark Side Of The Moon* album. The other guitar was a Gibson Les Paul TV that he used for a few of the following shows.

LEWIS, NOVEMBER 1970

During the Atom Heart Mother World Tour, Pink Floyd played on 7th October in Vancouver, Canada. While there, David visited a music shop and tried a custom guitar made by Bill Lewis, a well-known local guitar maker.

The Lewis guitar was unique as it had 24 frets, a full two-octave range (as opposed to the standard 21 frets on a Strat) and an extra-wide fingerboard. The guitar also featured Lewis's own type of Humbucker pickups that were selectable to single coil, producing a very clean sound. The guitar was made of Honduras mahogany with an ebony fretboard and had a removable back for access to the electronics.

The extra-wide fingerboard, which flattened out by the 24th fret, was supposed to be a great advantage for bending notes; however, David found that because it was perfectly flat, it was difficult to play the higher notes at the top end. The rubber-banded volume knob on the Lewis did provide a smooth feel and easy operation whilst playing which was very much to David's liking.

This led him to later replace the volume knob on the Black Strat with a similar one. This silver volume knob can be seen on the Black Strat during the Paris studio filming sessions for the *Pink Floyd: Live At Pompeii* film.

On 12th November 1970, Pink Floyd performed two shows at The Falkoner Centret in Copenhagen, Denmark with David using the Lewis. The set list included *Astronomy Domine, Fat Old Sun, Atom Heart Mother*, and *The Embryo*. The local paper (BT) reviewed the show, and wrote:

Pink Floyd at The Falconer Centret, Copenhagen, November 1970

"They impressed an audience of 3,800 people with their cosmic sound. They dominated their equipment to a scary degree."

During spring/summer of 1971 David used the Lewis to record some parts on the album *Meddle*. The following year he used it to play the latter part of the solo on *Money* for *The Dark Side Of The Moon* album.

In the early eighties, guitar maker Roger Giffin replaced the fingerboard on the Lewis with a slightly thicker convex one (it was too thin to reshape the original) to make it easier to play.

David can be seen playing the Lewis in Abbey Road Studio 2 on the Classic Albums *The Dark Side Of The Moon* documentary (2003).

The guitar was displayed at the Pink Floyd Interstellar Exhibition in Paris, France, in 2003-2004.

Above left: The Lewis guitar showing the removable back
Top: David at Abbey Road Studios – 'The Dark Side Of The Moon' recording sessions 1972
Above: David at Abbey Road Studios – 'The Dark Side Of The Moon' Documentary 2003

Right: Backstage at Ahoy Hall, Rotterdam, April 1971
Below: Crystal Palace Bowl, London, May 1971
Facing page clockwise from top left: Pink Floyd's inflatable octopus; David with the Black Strat at Ahoy Hall, Rotterdam April 1971; Using a steel bar during 'A Saucerful Of Secrets', Crystal Palace Bowl, London, May 1971; On stage at Crystal Palace Bowl, London, May 1971

4 BACK TO BLACK

Having experimented with other makes and models of guitars, David returned to the Black Strat as his main instrument.

Pink Floyd headlined the Garden Party concert at the Crystal Palace Bowl, London, on 15th May 1971. The Bowl stage was somewhat similar in design to the Hollywood Bowl and separated from the audience by a small lake. Support acts were The Faces, Mountain and Quiver. At this concert Pink Floyd used their Quadraphonic sound system outdoors with speakers situated around the rim of the arena. They performed their new piece, *Return Of The Son Of Nothing,* later renamed *Echoes,* which they had been working on since January. The climax of this outdoor show featured smoke bombs, rockets and a giant inflatable octopus rising out of the lake in front of the stage.

Throughout the rest of May, Pink Floyd performed in Scotland and England, also spending
five days in Abbey Road Studios, London for
some *Meddle* recording sessions.

A European tour followed with dates in
West Germany, Italy, England, The Netherlands,
Austria and France.

In June they played at the 13th century
Abbaye de Royaumont, just north of Paris.
Now home to the Royaumont French Cultural
Foundation, the show was recorded for broad-
cast in July (Cinq Grand Sur La Deux) by ORTF2
French television.

After these shows, further recording sessions for *Meddle* took place at Morgan Sound
Studios, London. Throughout this period, David
continued using his Black Strat.

Right: Abbaye de Royaumont, France 15th June 1971

Pink Floyd travelled to Japan and Australia for the first time in August 1971 for concerts in Hakone, Osaka, Melbourne, and Sydney. Their performance at the Open Air Festival in Hakone Aphrodite, Hakone, Japan on the 6th and 7th August was filmed by a local television crew, as was their performance at the Randwick Racecourse in Sydney, Australia on 15th August. In footage of both occasions, David can be seen playing his Black Strat. On returning to England the band had further recording dates for *Meddle* at both Air and Command Studios, London.

Left and below: Hakone Aphrodite, Japan, August 1971

THE BLACK STRAT AT POMPEII

From 4th to 7th October 1971, Pink Floyd staged a performance in the ancient Roman Amphitheatre, Pompeii, Italy. There was no audience, just director Adrian Maben with his crew filming the band performing *Echoes*, *Careful With That Axe Eugene*, *A Saucerful Of Secrets*, *One Of These Days I'm Going To Cut You Into Little Pieces*, and *Set The Controls For The Heart Of The Sun*.

The film, released to the cinema as *Pink Floyd: Live At Pompeii* (1972), featured the band playing in daylight, without any visual effects, in the centre

The Roman Amphitheatre at Pompeii, Italy, with Mount Vesuvius in the background

of the old empty amphitheatre. David can be seen playing his Black Strat conventionally, and somewhat less conventionally with it balanced on his lap while seated on the ground. Prior to the release of the film, additional footage was shot of Pink Floyd performing at the Studio Europasonor, Paris, in December and then at Abbey Road. This was later edited together with the outdoor scenes shot in and around Pompeii and at the amphitheatre.

Whilst in the studio, the band performed most of the same songs, adding *Mademoiselle Nobs*, with Roger playing the Black Strat, David on harmonica and Rick coaxing vocals from a local Borzoi.

Facing page top: Roger, David, singing Borzoi and Rick performing at the Studio Europasonor, Paris, December 1971
Facing page bottom: Pink Floyd playing in the amphitheatre at Pompeii, October 1971

Below: Roger Waters on the Black Strat with David on harmonica at the Studio Europasonor, Paris, December 1971
Bottom: Three stills from 'Pink Floyd: Live At Pompeii' show David playing the Black Strat in the amphitheatre at Pompeii, October 1971

SILVER VOLUME KNOB

The standard volume knob on the Black Strat was changed to a silver one between the Pompeii amphitheatre shoot and the footage from the Paris Studio. This was an attempt to replicate the feel of the volume knob on David's Lewis guitar, which had a rubber banding around its circumference. It made a subtle difference by making a more tactile, smoother and easier operation of the control whilst playing.

Top and above: Performing at the Studio Europasonor, Paris, December 1971
for the filming of 'Pink Floyd: Live At Pompeii' directed by Adrien Maben
Facing page: Adrian Maben gives directions to the band

5 BLACK VARIATIONS

On the 30th October 1971, *Meddle* was released to critical acclaim. Musically more cohesive than previous albums, it was recorded between January and August at Abbey Road Studios, Morgan Sound Studios, and AIR Studios in London. The album included *Echoes*, a twenty-two minute epic sound journey which featured David playing the Black Strat with his fluid guitar lines, funky rhythms, seagull calls and soaring leads.

The weekly music newspaper RECORD MIRROR (UK) reviewed the album:

"Marvellous long-awaited album from a recluse group that maintains its high regard with every release. Typically professional use of studio effects plus excellent musicianship. 'Fearless' is a superb track featuring electric guitar picking, steady drumming, and an ascending bass line. Terrific blend of acoustic guitar and electrics and added Liverpool football crowd chanting to end it. Pastiche howlin' blues includes doggy wailing on 'Seamus'. The whole of side 2 is taken with the symphonic scale of 'Echoes'. From mood to mood, rhythm to rhythm, an expertly devised musical life-cycle that will take you down, back up, in, around, through and leave you on your way into outer space. Their best album yet."

David used the Black Strat on Pink Floyd's subsequent tour of the US and Canada to promote *Meddle* in October and November. This included a spectacular concert at the Carnegie Hall, New York.

In early January, the band rehearsed for a new British tour at The Rolling Stones' warehouse studio in Bermondsey, London. It would feature a brand-new piece about the pressures and stresses of everyday life titled *Eclipse*. An early version was premiered on the first day of the tour at The Dome, Brighton, England. It consisted of the the songs *Breathe, On The Run* (with a guitar improvisation), *Time* (slow tempo), *The Mortality Sequence* (organ-based with preachers giving sermons in the background), *Money, Us And Them* (with a moaning intro), *Any Colour You Like* and *Brain Damage*.

Changing and adding songs, the new material was altered, re-worked and refined with each live performance. This early version of *The Dark Side Of The Moon* was developed and later recorded over the course of 1972.

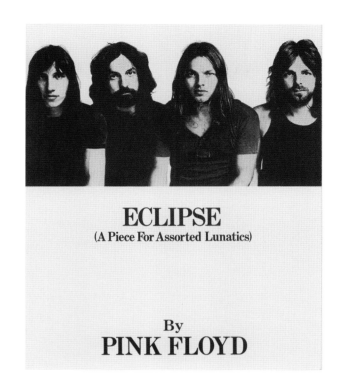

ECLIPSE
(A Piece For Assorted Lunatics)

By
PINK FLOYD

MODIFICATIONS TO THE BLACK STRAT

Top: XLR Socket
Above: Additional black
selector switch
Circled:The XLR hole is still
visible at The Rainbow,
London, February 1972

Over the years, David has considered the Black Strat to be his 'working guitar', the instrument that he would use to test new ideas. Always willing to alter it in the quest for improvement, many different modifications have been made to the guitar. These include the fitting of six different necks, several pickups and a number of other changes.

XLR SOCKET

One of the first alterations made to the guitar after fitting the silver volume knob was to fit an XLR socket. David drilled out the wooden body and fitted the socket to the side of the guitar and an additional selector switch to the pickguard. The socket was positioned below the original output jack socket. It was installed to send the guitar signal to drive the input of a fuzz box with the maximum signal level – in order for it to operate correctly. The signal then went back into the guitar (selectable with the switch) to enable the guitar volume control to be used as a master volume. This modification failed to achieve the desired result. David soon removed the XLR socket and some time later, with a secret mixture he concocted of sawdust and glue, repaired the hole where the XLR had been and retouched the black paint.

NOISE REDUCTION

Over time, changes have been made to the guitar to improve the sound quality and eliminate as much unwanted noise as possible. These include the ground being rewired and copper foil fitted with additional earth points (*see below*) to improve the shielding.

TUNERS

The fitted Fender 'F' style tuners that were introduced in the late 60's were not of the same quality as the earlier Kluson type previously used by Fender. The gearing was a little slack and less positive, consequently accurate tuning was more difficult so David replaced them with Schallers.

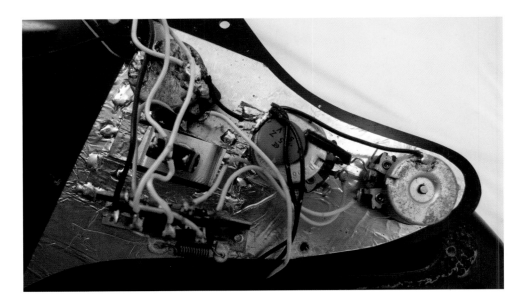

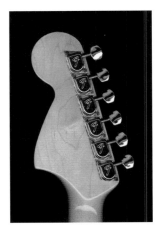

Right: Schaller tuners,
Rainbow Theatre, 1972
Far right: Fender tuners

A NEW BLACK STRAT WITH BULLET
TRUSS ROD, 1972

In early 1972, David began using a brand new black Fender Stratocaster with a maple neck and white pickguard. This was the third black Strat that he had purchased at Manny's Music over the last two years whilst on tours in the US.

This guitar was one of Fender's latest models and featured a micro-tilt neck with a bullet truss rod adjustment. This allowed access to the truss rod at the top of the neck behind the nut. This feature was designed to make truss rod adjustments much easier than on the older necks. It got its 'bullet' name from the silver nut at the top of the neck that looked similar to a silver bullet.

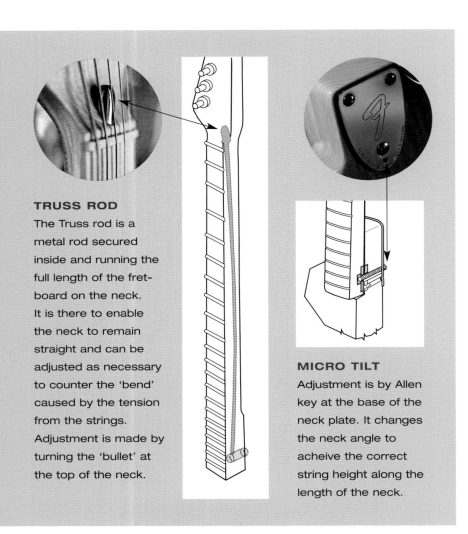

TRUSS ROD

The Truss rod is a metal rod secured inside and running the full length of the fretboard on the neck. It is there to enable the neck to remain straight and can be adjusted as necessary to counter the 'bend' caused by the tension from the strings. Adjustment is made by turning the 'bullet' at the top of the neck.

MICRO TILT

Adjustment is by Allen key at the base of the neck plate. It changes the neck angle to acheive the correct string height along the length of the neck.

48

Bullet Strat, Rainbow Theatre,
London, February 1972

Despite the fact that this guitar was one of the latest models, it was not David's favourite. The neck was attached to the body using three bolts instead of four, as on older models, making it impossible to interchange his necks. This guitar was used intermittently over the next year or so, mainly as a spare, before it eventually underwent a modification.

David did not like the style and look of the large headstock Fender were now using, as compared to the smaller vintage style of the rosewood neck. He attempted to correct this 'look' by using a jigsaw to remodel the shape of the headstock to a more vintage style (this was not considered a great success), the guitar was not seen again. The pickup assembly was removed and later fitted to the Black Strat.

THE DARK SIDE OF THE MOON
PRESS PREMIERE, FEBRUARY 1972

From the 17th to the 20th February, Pink Floyd felt confident enough with their new material to hold a press premiere of *The Dark Side Of The Moon* at the Rainbow Theatre, London. David used his Black Strat, fitted with the silver volume knob and extra selector switch, for these shows as well as the new bullet Strat.

THE NEW MUSICAL EXPRESS reviewed the concerts:

"At the last of their four sell-out nights at the London Rainbow, they opened the show with their new hour-long piece *The Dark Side Of The Moon*, an assault on the corruption of media, delivered, ironically enough, with all the facilities of media at their disposal; gigantic light towers; banks of quadraphonic speakers; taped harangues from Muggeridge and his ilk; all swirling, floating and moving from space to space, leaving the listener stunned and yet not bewildered. At the end of the piece, police sirens echoed through the Rainbow, revolving red lights atop the speaker- banks were switched on, and the main light tower – to the accompaniment of agonized mechanical groans – dipped in mock salute to media, to Floyd, and to us. Tremendous. I have literally never heard such good-quality sound in any auditorium from any group – ever. It's been almost eighteen months since I last saw Pink Floyd, and I'd forgotten how unbelievable they can be. I won't forget again. Honest, Eugene."

'The Dark Side Of The Moon' Press Premiere, Rainbow Theatre, London, February 1972
Below left and following page: The Black Strat
Below: The bullet Strat

OBSCURED BY CLOUDS, 1972

Wedged between *Meddle* and *The Dark Side Of The Moon*, Pink Floyd released *Obscured By Clouds*. The bands second outing as composers for a Barbet Schroeder film (the first being *More*), the material consisted of music for the soundtrack to the movie *La Vallée*.

Either side of a Japanese tour, the songs had been hastily written and recorded during two one-week periods in February and March in the Strawberry Studio at the Château d'Herouville, near Paris. It contained excellent harmonies between David and Rick Wright, both vocally and instrumentally. David used the Black Strat and the bullet Strat for a range of guitar sounds, from slide to fuzz-tone, and with a wah-wah giving an almost vocal-like quality. Despite the hectic recording schedule, the album contains some powerfully sublime moments and received praise from the critics. DISC & MUSIC ECHO called it "an amazing album".

Below: Outside the Strawberry Studio at the Château d'Herouville, near Paris

Above: David playing the double neck guitar,
Detroit, Michigan, April 1972
Below: The double neck body
Right: Dick Knight

A DOUBLE NECK EXPERIMENT, MARCH 1972

A Boeing DC8 was hired to take the band, crew, equipment, family and friends for a brief one-week tour in Japan. This long flight provided an ideal opportunity for David to spend some time considering the assembly of a double neck Strat. He had just received the double neck body from Dick Knight, the guitar maker, who had made it from a mahogany plank that David had previously delivered. Dick was asked to make a double Strat body that would accommodate two separate six-string Strat necks, tremolos and electronics.

David began by removing the necks from the Black Strat and the sunburst Strat to see how they would fit on the double body. This would help to give him an idea as to how the guitar would ultimately work. The double-neck Strat was an experiment, the idea was to be able to quickly change between playing conventional and slide guitar (requiring the strings to be set to a higher action so the steel bar does not hit the frets).

The construction was completed at a later date and the double neck was used sparingly at shows on the US tour in April and May. Despite the extra versatility the double neck promised, it proved to be too cumbersome and heavy to use on stage. It was abandoned as unsuccessful shortly thereafter.

Above: The double neck body as it is today shown with the rosewood neck from the white (now natural) Strat and the Charvel 22 fret neck

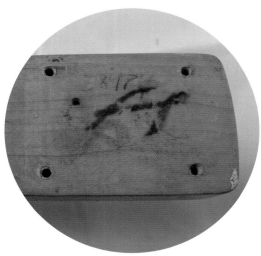

REFITTING THE BLACK STRAT WITH A ROSEWOOD NECK, JUNE 1972

David had been using a number of different guitars. The double neck Strat was heavy and impractical, and he wasn't keen on the design of the bullet Strat.

He returned to the Black Strat, which underwent a significant change. Despite preferring maple necks, having used them side-by-side on the double body, the rosewood neck had a nicer profile and feel with a preferable smaller

Right: The Black Strat fitted with the 1963 rosewood neck from the sunburst Strat

56

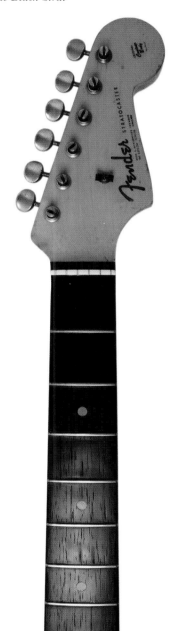

vintage headstock. He decided to disassemble the double neck, swapping the original maple neck from the Black Strat with the rosewood neck from the sunburst Strat. The serial number plates from the two guitars were also exchanged along with their necks. The Black Strat was reassembled without the silver volume knob and additional pickup selector switch.

THE DARK SIDE OF THE MOON
JUNE 1972/FEBRUARY 1973

Although Pink Floyd had toured an early version of the piece, *Eclipse* - in January, it wasn't until the end of May that the actual recording of *The Dark Side Of The Moon* began at Abbey Road Studio 3, London. After taking a three-month break for various concerts and holidays, the recording recommenced in October. The album was finally completed in early February 1973.

During these sessions David primarily used the Black Strat for his visceral guitar solos, rhythm parts and fills with a variety of different effects, which included using a uni-vibe and playing through a Leslie revolving speaker. He provided his own imitable flair and style to the music, rooted in blues and notable for expressive note bends and sustain – particularly in his guitar solo on *Time*. A combination of guitars was used for *Money*, on which the first two solos were recorded with the Black Strat and the third with the Lewis.

Reviews from The Dark Side Of The Moon tour:

"From the word go, they gave the packed arena a faultless demonstration of what psychedelic music is all about. There wasn't a note, or a sound out of place during the whole evening. It's a recital more than a concert, and the Floyd don't so much give us numbers as perform pieces of music. The lighting tower belched out smoke which mingled with the coloured lights and the dry ice surface mist to effectively whisk us all away to Planet Floyd."

SOUNDS

"The Dark Side Of The Moon was 'stunning' with smoking lighting towers, quadraphonic sound, flash pots, and a flaming gong".

MELODY MAKER

THE DOME, BRIGHTON, JUNE 1972

The Black Strat, now with the rosewood neck, was first used live on the 28th and 29th June at The Dome, Brighton, England. At these shows, the audience heard the complete live version of *The Dark Side Of The Moon* for the first time.

    The Black Strat had now become David's instrument of choice. The rosewood neck would remain on it until 1978, when it was replaced with a Charvel neck prior to *The Wall.*

U.S. TOUR, SEPTEMBER 1972

In September, Pink Floyd began their seventh tour of the United States, playing to larger audiences than ever before. In Los Angeles, they performed at the prestigious Hollywood Bowl, a large open-air amphitheatre. In addition to their usual lighting, theatrical smoke and fire effects, they had eight powerful searchlights spectacularly fanning their beams skyward from behind the domed stage into the night sky. Followed by a colourful firework display as the finale, a fantastic show in a beautiful setting.

For this show, David primarily used his Black Strat, which had recently been fitted with an additional pickup switch. The sunburst Strat was used for slide guitar on *One Of These Days.*

Hollywood Bowl, September 1972

Right and below: Wembley, London, October 1972 The hole where the XLR has been removed is still visible behind the guitar cable. The additional pick up selector switch has been reinstated

EXTRA PICKUP SELECTOR SWITCH

David reinstalled a second selector switch on the pickguard of his Black Strat. He wired it to allow the neck pickup to be used simultaneously with either the bridge or middle pickup, offering him the choice of a different sound. This combination was not available with the stock pickup selector on Fender Stratocaster guitars, and whilst this has now become a standard modification, at the time it was an innovative idea.

Wembley, London, October 1972. David playing the sunburst Strat with the Black Strat leaning against the amplifiers

WEMBLEY EMPIRE POOL, OCTOBER 1972

Pink Floyd interrupted their *The Dark Side Of The Moon* recording sessions during October to perform at three benefit concerts for The War on Want, The Albany Trust Deptford and Save the Children Fund at the Wembley Empire Pool, London. Dick Parry had recorded his saxophone part on *Money* the week before and was invited to play it live on stage one of the nights. These concerts featured David using both the Black Strat with the rosewood neck and the sunburst Strat with the maple neck.

EUROPEAN TOUR, NOVEMBER/DECEMBER 1972

A European tour followed in November and December including dates in Denmark, West Germany, France, Belgium and Switzerland. The set list follows the pattern for the year with *The Dark Side Of The Moon* in its entirety as the first half of the show. This tour also marked the last shows where the old arrangements of *On The Run* and *The Great Gig In The Sky* were played. These tracks would be changed by the following March when the album was released. David predominately used the Black Strat during this tour, with the bullet Strat as his second guitar (and for slide). Between these European dates, the band rehearsed and performed with the Ballets de Marseille, directed and choreographed by eminent avant-garde Roland Petit.

Palais des Sports, Toulouse, November 1972

ADDING A HUMBUCKER PICKUP JANUARY 1973

Right: David's original Humbucker – now removed Facing page: The original Humbucker pickup placed back in situ. Note: David has removed the wood between the bridge and middle pickup cavities to accommodate the pickup. Extra wood has been removed to allow the eccentrically shaped Strat middle pickup to be reversed, to create enough room for the humbucker between the bridge and middle pickups.

Early in 1973 David fitted an additional pickup to the Black Strat, a Gibson 'Patent Number' Humbucker which he had previously acquired. This pickup has two coils and produces a fatter or higher output signal than the single coil, as is standard on Strats. He thought it would be interesting to try it on his Black Strat. The new Humbucker was installed between the original bridge and middle pickups, requiring the guitar's body to be routed out to accommodate it, and the pickguard modified to fit. The second selector switch was now used to select the Humbucker.

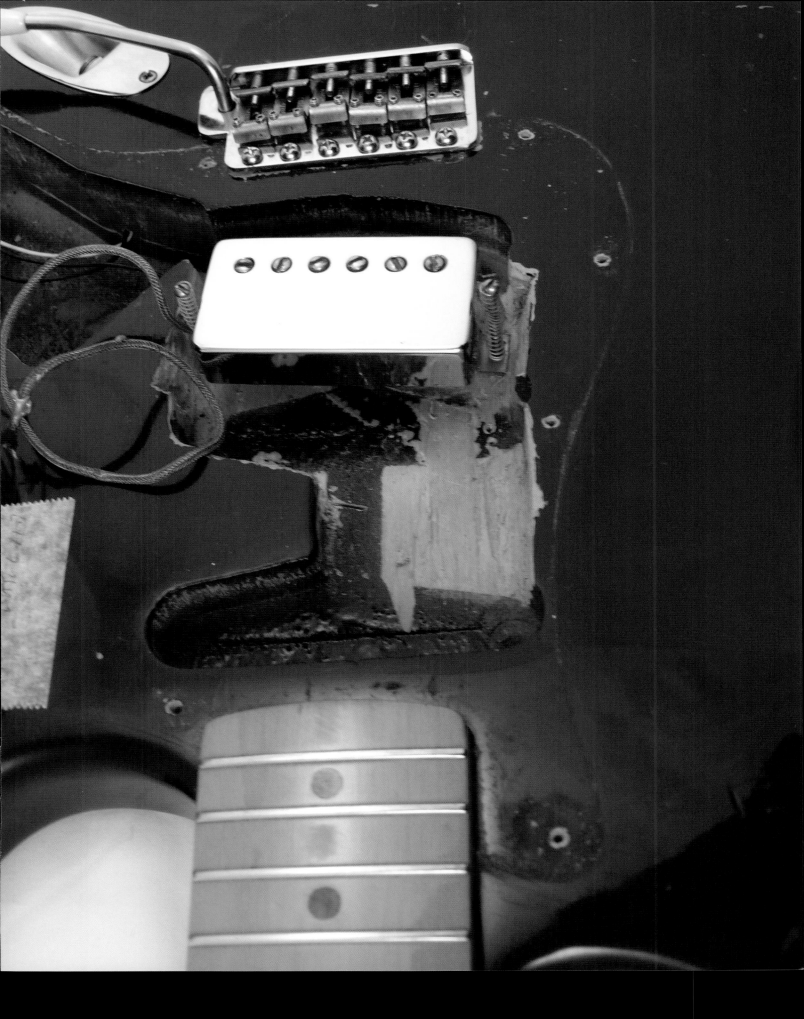

The Black Strat, fitted with a new Humbucker, returned to France as Pink Floyd performed further shows in January and February accompanying the Ballets de Marseille. These performances were at the Palais des Sports de la Porte de Versailles, Paris. With a programme they had performed at various times throughout the year predominately as the second half of their live act, Pink Floyd played *One Of These Days, Careful With That Axe Eugene, Obscured By Clouds, When You're In* and *Echoes*. David used the Black Strat, with the bullet Strat as a slide guitar. Between these performances the band returned to Abbey Road Studios to complete the album they had been working on sporadically over the past months, *The Dark Side Of The Moon*.

Engineer Alan Parsons notes,

"Gilmour took several hours to prepare his guitar sounds for each track, but then recorded straightforwardly with one microphone, very fast and at 'wall shaking' volume". So relaxed were they that, "they produced each other – Roger would produce David playing guitar and singing and David would produce Roger doing his vocals".

Above and left: David is playing the Black Strat with added Humbucker pickup. The bullet Strat is leaning against the amplifiers

Far right: January 12, 1973, rehearsing the Ballets de Marseille at the Palais des Sports de la Porte de Versailles, Paris

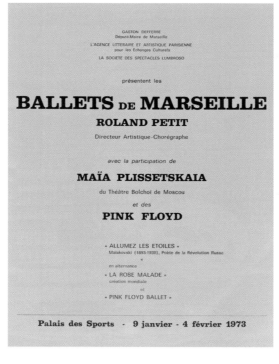

69

THE DARK SIDE OF THE MOON, US TOUR
MARCH 1973

Above: Kent State University, Ohio, March 1973
Bottom right: The Humbucker is visible under David's hand, the XLR hole is still un-repaired

On the 4th March in Madison, Wisconsin, Pink Floyd began another US tour. The show included their new album, *The Dark Side Of The Moon*, released on the 10th March in the US and the 23rd March in the UK.

In addition to the four band members, for the first time, the touring ensemble included female backing vocalists. The Black Strat with the Humbucker pickup was used throughout the tour and the final show was on the 24th March in Atlanta, Georgia.

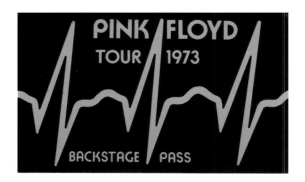

MUSIC HAL
260 TREMONT ST., BOSTON,

T 104
ORCHESTRA
CNTR

MARCH
14
1973

Wed. Eve. a
RON DELSE
— PRESENTS
PINK FLO.
ADMISSION $6.

EARLS COURT BENEFIT CONCERTS MAY 1973

On the 18th and 19th May, Pink Floyd played two benefit shows for SHELTER (National Campaign for the Homeless) at the Earls Court Exhibition Hall, London. Pink Floyd's 'Hi-Fi', crystal clear quadraphonic sound seemed almost alive as it travelled around this massive arena. The audience experienced the band performing *The Dark Side Of The Moon* live for the first time in England since the release of the album. The abundance of spectacular visual effects were stunning: Strobe lights appeared from the drum-kit, blinding white searchlights scanned the arena, an aircraft flew the length of the hall, rockets shot

into the air, fireworks exploded, the gong burst into flames and industrial quantities of dry ice created a surreal and atmospheric mood. The band had continued to set the benchmark by which other shows would be judged.

For the first time saxophonist Dick Parry joined the female backing vocalists as part of the touring entourage. David used both his Black Strat with the Humbucker and the bullet Strat for these performances.

"People are always saying 'This is the best gig ever' so I won't bother. But Floyd's nights at Earl's Court were rock theatre at its best, music at its finest – and if that ain't enough the proceeds were donated to Shelter. There's a spirit in the sky."

Steve Clarke, NME

Earls Court Benefit Concert,
May 1973
Below: David playing the Black
Strat with the bullet Strat
leaning against the amplifiers
Far right top: David playing the
Black Strat with Humbucker
Far right bottom: The bullet Strat

RETURNING TO STANDARD PICKUPS, 1973

The band returned to the US for a short tour starting in New Jersey on 16th June and finishing in Tampa, Florida, on 29th June. David decided to return the Black Strat to original standard electronics. Preferring the clearer sound of original single coil pickups, he removed the complete pickup assembly on the modified white pickguard with the added Humbucker and extra switch from the Black Strat. He replaced these with the standard set taken from the 're-modeled' black bullet Strat.

Below: Rear view of middle pick-up, date code 8022 from the bullet Strat
Bottom: Rear view of pots, date code 7112 (12th week 1971) from the bullet Strat

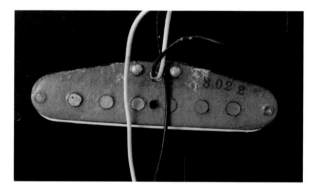

Facing page and left: Robert Wyatt Benefit concert at The Rainbow Theatre, London, November 1973

NOVEMBER 1973

On the 4th November, Pink Floyd made a special guest appearance to play a benefit concert with Soft Machine for their drummer Robert Wyatt - a friend of the band who had suffered a near fatal accident leaving him paralyzed from the waist down. Two shows were performed that evening, 5pm and 9pm, at The Rainbow Theatre, London, raising a considerable sum for Robert's rehabilitation. They played *The Dark Side Of The Moon*, along with the songs *Obscured By Clouds* and *When You're In*.

MELODY MAKER reported:

> "Pink Floyd stunned fans with two sensational shows at London's Rainbow Theatre on Sunday night. Combining quadraphonic pre-recorded tapes, lights, smoke and theatrical effects into a kind of Son et Lumiere… the audience rose to give them an ovation. They deserved a Nobel prize or at least an Oscar".

FRENCH TOUR, JUNE 1974

The last time that David played the Black Strat fitted with a white pickguard was during a brief French tour between the 18th and 26th June. The final shows were at the Palais des Sports de la Porte de Versailles, Paris. These performances marked the first time that Pink Floyd used a circular screen.

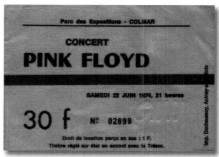

This added a new and significant visual dimension to the shows. The screen was hung behind the band and utilised rear projection for their specially commissioned films and animation to accompany some of the music from *Meddle* and *The Dark Side Of The Moon*.

Right: David at home 1974
Facing page: Hyde Park,
August 1974, Guest
appearance with
Roy Harper

6 THE ALL BLACK

ADDING A BLACK PICKGUARD, SUMMER 1974

In the summer of 1974, David installed an all black pickguard on the Black Strat. It was first seen in public when he made a guest appearance with Roy Harper on 31st August at the free concert in Hyde Park, London. He also used the Black Strat to record *The Game* in Abbey Road Studio 3, London, on Roy's album *HQ*.

In October, he used the all Black Strat during tour rehearsal/writing sessions at Unit Studio in Kings Cross, London. It was there that David, out of the blue, played the four note guitar figure which was the inspiration for *Shine On You Crazy Diamond*. Two other songs, *Raving* and *Drooling*, later reworked as *Sheep*, and *You Gotta Be Crazy*, later to be recorded as *Dogs*, were also written during this three-week period.

These songs formed the first half of the show for the British winter tour in November and December, followed by *The Dark Side Of The Moon* with *Echoes* as an encore.

Right: British winter tour, 1974
Below: Performing 'Echoes' as an encore during the British winter tour, 1974
Facing page: Hyde Park, August 1974

WISH YOU WERE HERE, 1975

With public expectations high after the global success of *The Dark Side Of The Moon*, recording sessions for a new album took place from January to March, and later in May to July at Abbey Road Studio 3 for a new album.

After a week in the studio, David was trying to get the right sound for the four-note guitar figure, his intro into *Shine On You Crazy Diamond*. He realised that Studio 1, the huge recording room normally reserved and frequented by orchestras, was currently unoccupied. Here was an opportunity to experiment and record his guitar part within a large, live ambient room. The guitar equipment was swiftly removed from Studio 3 and taken down the staircase. With David as both the instigator and assistant roadie, it was redeployed at the far end of the cavernous Studio 1.

He played the Black Strat through a Binson Echorec 2 delay unit amplified by a Fender Dual Showman amp with a 2×15 cabinet, a Hiwatt amp with a WEM 4×12 cabinet and a Leslie 760 rotating speaker cabinet.

Beginning and ending with the Syd Barrett tribute, *Shine On You Crazy Diamond*, released on the 30th July as *Wish You Were Here*, the album received critical acclaim. Aside from the classic acoustic title track, David predominately used the Black Strat. He contributed haunting and emotive guitar parts both during the making of the album and for the live shows.

Facing page top: Abbey Road, Studio 1: David recording guitar intro to 'Shine On Your Crazy Diamond', Phil (right)
Facing page bottom: Abbey Road: Daily work sheet

86

RECORDING SHEET

Job No. 57199 P

ARTISTIC INFORMATION			COSTING INFORMATION	

Dolby		Artist			Date	21st · Jan 75.	Session Booked Time	2.30 — 12	Materials Used

Dolby: 24T / 16T / 8T / 4T / 2T / Mono / Quad.

Artist: PINK FLOY(D)

Date: 21st · Jan 75.
Location: Studio 3
Engineers: BcL/PJ
Producer: PINK FLOYD

Session Booked Time: 2.30 — 12
Recording/SI: 2.30 — 10.45
Remixing: ✓
Copying: ✓
Playback: ½ hr   **Editing:** AA 1 hr
Materials Used: ~~8 (2)~~

REEL NOS.	TITLES	False Starts	Take Nos.	From	To	DUR.	REMARKS
7820/(24 T)	SHINE ON YOU CRAZY DIAMOND		6	—	—		
		7	8	B/D,			
	Outro part.						
818/(24 T)	Part 2			Superimposition s/Gtr (with No 1 Studio) (5 — 7.30 pm)			
				Pt 1 - 6 Edited together on 7818/(24 T)			
	" " " "			Superimposition of Rhythm Gtr.			

Ref. No 9864A   Abbey Road

Right:US Tour 1975
Below: Abbey Road, Studio 3:
Recording

Knebworth July 1975

Two North American three-week tours in April and June had been undertaken between the Abbey Road recording dates.

Returning to England to headline a concert in the grand setting of Knebworth Park on 5th July, Pink Floyd were supported by The Steve Miller Band, Captain Beefheart and Roy Harper. With great effect, the band started their set with a fly past by two original Spitfires low over the crowd. This was the last time that they would play *The Dark Side Of The Moon* in its entirety until 1994.

ANIMALS, 1976/77
DIMARZIO PICKUP

Between April and November, Pink Floyd recorded *Animals* at their newly
built recording studio situated within their sound and lighting equipment
warehouse at 35 Britannia Row, Islington, North London.
Custom pickups were uncommon in 1976 and David had acquired
a DiMarzio FS-1 pickup to try in the Black Strat. He
preferred the sound of the DiMarzio, when installed in
the bridge position, to the original stock Fender pickup.
The newly modified Black Strat was used during the
recording and on the ensuing Animals tour from January
through July 1977 across Europe and the US.

    After the melancholy beauty of *Wish You Were Here*, this
album had an edgier and more aggressive sound. Powerful,
dramatic, dynamic and moody, David played some masterful
rhythm and lead guitar. It was also the first time he used a talkbox
with the Black Strat. *Animals* was released on 21st January, 1977.

*Facing page: Empire Pool,
Wembley, London, March 1977
Below: The original DiMarzio
pickup and the Fender pickup
it replaced*

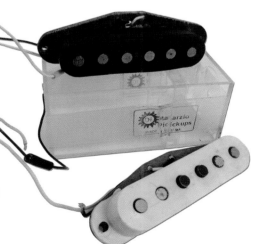

David with the Black Strat and Phil on stage testing
his equipment prior to the first US Animals show,
Baseball Stadium, Miami, April 1977

DAVID GILMOUR, 1978

David released his eponymous solo debut, *David Gilmour*, in May 1978. It was recorded at Pink Floyd's Britannia Row Studio, London and at Superbear Studio, France in late '77 early '78, mainly as a trio with Rick Wills and Willie Wilson – the same line-up as his pre Pink Floyd band Bullitt from 1967. It reflects David's blues influences with a Floyd flavour, using the Black Strat to create his signature guitar sound. The album contains some impressive solos, excellent vocals and superb lap steel work.

A promotional film was shot at The Roxy, London. The film features David playing the Black Strat along with his brother Mark Gilmour (guitar), Rick Wills (bass guitar), Willie Wilson (drums), and Ian McLagan (keyboards).

> "... the Stratocaster that I use on stage with the Pink Floyd, which is the same one that I use quite a bit on the solo album, is....the neck is from an early sixties Strat, the body is about 1970, and the electrics are from the same time. It's got a DiMarzio pickup for the treble, but I don't think that makes that much difference - it's quite nice, I also use another Strat that is perfectly standard (sunburst with maple neck). It's mostly between three guitars - two Stratocasters and one Telecaster/Esquire."
>
> *David Gilmour interview,* BEAT INSTRUMENTAL, July 1978

Right: Recording Engineer John Etchells with David at Superbear Studio, France in early 1978
Facing page: Filming at the Roxy, London 1978
Top: Willie Wilson, David and Rick Wills (left to right)
Bottom: Joanne Stone, Vicki Brown, Liza Strike, Mark Gilmour, David, Willie Wilson, Rick Wills, Ian McLaagan (left to right)

CHANGING TO A CHARVEL NECK, ADDING A SECOND SWITCH, AUTUMN 1978

The rosewood neck on the Black Strat was getting slightly worn and David's preference was maple. In December 1977, a new birds eye maple neck was ordered from Grover Jackson, who had recently purchased Charvel's guitar

parts supply company and had begun making guitars. Given the specifications, he made this custom neck with a thicker truss rod and a Fender decal on the headstock. It was fitted to the guitar in late summer 1978.

A small recessed toggle switch was added to the pickguard between the volume knob and the pickup selector switch, allowing the neck pickup to be used with the bridge or middle pickups. This modification performed the same function as the similar switch that was previously added by David in 1972.

The original rosewood neck was now refitted onto the sunburst Strat.

Above and right: Rear view of the mini toggle switch and mounting bracket
Facing page: Mini toggle switch between the volume knob and pickup selector

The Black Strat with
Charvel neck and the
sunburst Strat with
original rosewood neck
during the recording of
'The Wall', 1978/79
Facing page: Showing
wear on the front and
back of the rosewood neck

THE WALL, 1978/1981
SEYMOUR DUNCAN PICKUP

Pink Floyd recorded their next album, *The Wall*, between October 1978 and October 1979. Engineered by James Guthrie, the recording sessions began at their Britannia Row Studio, London, then relocated to Superbear Studio in the south of France and on to Producers Workshop in Los Angeles.

This concept album topped the charts on both sides of the Atlantic, provided Pink Floyd with their first number one single in America and became the largest selling double-disc album of all time. It contains some great guitar work, for which David used several different instruments, the main one being the Black Strat on which he played his now legendary solo in Comfortably Numb (voted the greatest guitar solo of all time by Planet Rock).

In late 1979, Seymour Duncan sent a custom pickup for David to try in the Black Strat. He preferred the sound of this new bridge pickup to the DiMarzio. It was permanently installed, first used on The Wall shows, and remains in the Black Strat to this day.

Facing page top left: Underside of Seymour Duncan and Fender pickups
Facing page bottom: 'The Wall' production rehearsal in the Sports Arena, Los Angeles, 1980

Invoice

SEYMOUR DUNCAN MFG.
box 4746 santa barbara, ca. 93103
(805) 962-6294

DATE June 27, 1979

№ 003877

SOLD TO
David Gilmore
Phil Taylor

Pink Floyd Music
35 Brittania Row
London N1 England

SHIPPED TO

YOUR ORDER NO.	DATE SHIPPED	SHIPPED VIA	F.O.B. POINT	SALESMAN	TERMS
ver	7/23/79	Emory-Rainbow Freight	SB	H	NO CHARGE

QUANTITY	DESCRIPTION	UNIT PRICE	TOTAL AMOUNT
3	SSL-1C Vintage staggered strats, custom	36 00	n/c
1	STL-3 Quarter Pound Tele lead	42 00	n/c
1	SSL-4 Quarter Pound Strat	42 00	n/c
1	SSL-1 Vintage Staggered strat	36 00	n/c
	SHIPPING		pre paid
	TOTAL		no charge

Seymour says hi and that he hopes you enjoy the pickups. Please let us know when you get over here. He always has his eye out for more guitars for you.

Thank You

ORIGINAL

FORM NO. 1N14N. THE STATIONERY HOUSE, INC., 1000 FLORIDA AVE. HAGERSTOWN MD. 21740

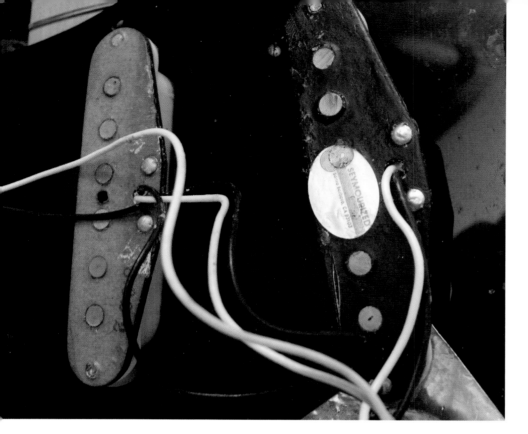

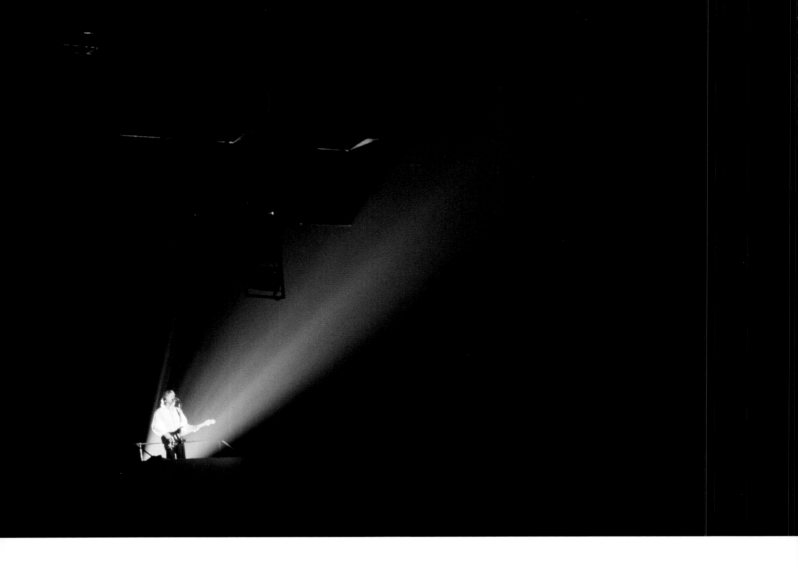

Above: For 'Comfortably Numb', a show highlight, David stood atop the wall playing his Black Strat
Facing page: Backstage view of David atop The Wall
Following pages: Nassau Coliseum, New York, February 1980, 'The Wall' show, intermission

The Wall live show was so large and complex that it was logistically impractical to attempt a normal tour. It was only performed for a week at a time in Los Angeles, New York and London in 1980, and again in Dortmund and London in 1981.

"Goodness knows what the psychologists would make of the vision of personal hell laid before us first with a startlingly brilliant album late last year and now, with the brutal inspiration of Gerald Scarfe and the mighty technology pioneered by Pink Floyd, turned into the most extravagant live show ever seen in London".

" In the finest coup de theatre of all, Gilmour is plucked out by the spotlights, singing and playing his own enthralling composition, 'Comfortably Numb', from the top of this colossal expanse of white."

THE DAILY TELEGRAPH

Facing page
Top: *Black pickguard cut out to accommodate the 22nd fret*
Bottom: *Charvel neck showing the 22nd fret overhang*

pink
floyd
the
final
cut

THE FINAL CUT, 1982
CHANGING TO A 22-FRET CHARVEL NECK

Early in the year, Pink Floyd planned to record *The Wall* movie soundtrack album. Due to differing points of view over material, these sessions ultimately resulted in a new studio album as opposed to the original plan. Recorded between July and December, the album was released as *The Final Cut*.

The guitar parts were recorded at David's Hook End Studio in Oxfordshire, Mayfair and Rak Studios, London. He played the Black Strat with a recently fitted custom Charvel 22 fret birds eye maple neck. Replacing the standard 21 fret neck, the new neck had a flatter radius and an extra fret – enabling him to play a semitone higher at the top end. Finished with button polish to give a nice feel, it had a Fender decal and Kluson tuners.

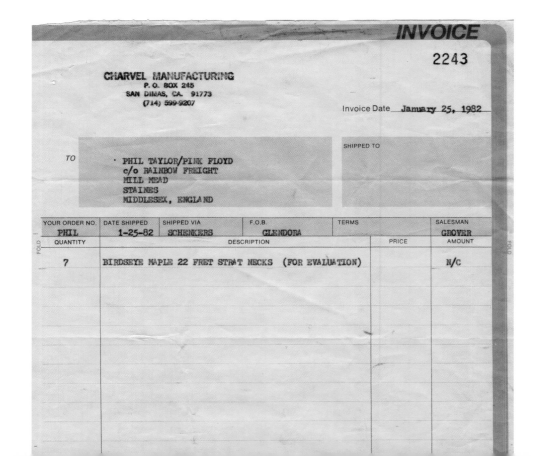

7 RETIRING THE BLACK

A NEW TREMOLO BRIDGE

The Kahler tremelo bridge

In 1983 a new tremolo system was fitted to the Black Strat. Designed by Dave Storey, this new form of tremolo bridge enabled the player to bend the string pitch further, and yet return back perfectly in tune as the strings were locked in position. In order to fit the system to David's Black Strat, a section of wood from behind the original bridge had to be removed from the body. At the time, no thought was given to how, or if, this might affect the sound of the guitar.

ABOUT FACE, 1984

The Black Strat, now sporting the 22-fret Charvel neck, a Kahler tremolo system and a new set of Gotoh tuners was taken to Pathé Marconi Studios, Paris in August 1983 and used to cut the tracks for David's new solo album *About Face*, with Jeff Porcaro (drums), Pino Palladino (Bass) and Ian Kewley (Keyboards).

Returning to England to complete the album, it features special guests including Steve Winwood, Ray Cooper and Roy Harper with Michael Kamen's superb orchestrations blending beautifully with David's Black Strat on the instrumental *Let's Get Metaphysical*.

In Pathé Marconi Studio, Paris, 1983

SHORTENED TREMOLO ARMS

During this time the tremolo arms on some of David's guitars were cut down in length. This was to enable the arm to rest more comfortably in the palm of his hand for a more sensitive response and better control while playing.

David's shortened and standard tremolo arms (actual size)

NEW STRATS

Under new ownership, Fender introduced a 1957 vintage reissue model Stratocaster. Interested in trying one out, David went to Arbiters warehouse in North London (the UK Fender distributor). He selected a few guitars that felt comfortable to play, acoustically sounded good and rang nicely.

A cream Strat immediately became his favourite and was used as his main guitar on the About Face tour, beginning in England in March and continuing through- out Europe and North America until July.

The Black Strat, now fitted with a bone nut and gold Gotoh tuners was still used for a few songs on the tour, with a dropped D tuning.

Another of these new guitars, a 57V candy-apple red Strat, was also used on the About Face tour, later to replace the cream Strat as his guitar of choice. These guitars were standard models, with the exception of the modified tremolo arms.

Facing page: With Mick Ralphs at the Muziekcentrum Vredenberg, Utrecht, The Netherlands, April 1984
Below: Hammersmith Odeon April 1984. Cream Strat

RED '57V STRAT WITH EMG PICKUPS 1985/2006

RF interference had, at times, been a problem as Pink Floyd continued to push the boundaries of what was possible. The lighting and visual effects, whilst appearing spectacular, were at times somewhat rudimentary in construction. Coupled with inadequate power sources and grounding, it often created RF interference problems for audio. Picked up and amplified by David's Fender single coil pickups and further worsened by his guitar effects with high gain stages, this resulted in an unacceptable level of unpleasant noise through the guitar amplifiers. To eliminate this, after the About Face tour, the red Strat (now established as his main guitar) and the cream were fitted with pickups specifically designed to eliminate noise. Low impedance active EMG-SA's were installed with two additional tone circuits, an EXG and an SPC replaced the original tone pots.

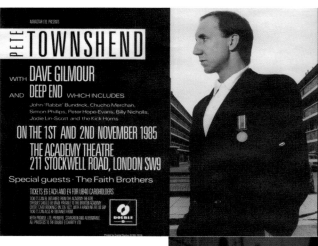

With Pete Townshend's Deep End 1986 for 'The Tube', television show

Live Aid, Wembley Stadium, London, July 1985

On 13th July 1985 David played the red Strat while accompanying Bryan Ferry for Live Aid at Wembley Stadium, London. A multi-venue concert organised to raise funds for famine relief in Ethiopia. The red Strat was also used for performances with Pete Townshend's Deep End on 'The Tube' television show, for concerts at London's Brixton Academy in November, and at Midem, Cannes, France, in February 1986.

THE BLACK STRAT AT THE HARD ROCK CAFÉ

In August 1986 a request was made, via Nick Mason, from the Hard Rock Café to obtain one of David's guitars for display. In return, they would

make a donation to The Nordoff-Robbins Music Therapy Centre Charity. As it was not currently being used, and it was for charity, he agreed to loan them his Black Strat on a semi-permanent basis, to be returned upon request. The appropriate paperwork was drawn up and the Black Strat was shipped to America where it was displayed in the Hard Rock Cafe in Dallas, Texas.

A MOMENTARY LAPSE OF REASON, 1987

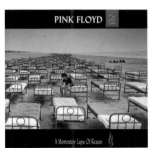

In 1987, after a six year absence, Pink Floyd returned to form with their first post-Waters album, *A Momentary Lapse Of Reason*. Recording began at Astoria, David's new houseboat studio, before decamping and continuing in Los Angeles. The red Strat was the main guitar used during these sessions.

Released on 8th September 1987, *A Momentary Lapse Of Reason* was a critical and commercial success and Pink Floyd undertook a world tour to promote the album. The tour started in Ottawa, Canada in September and ended in August 1988 with five nights at Nassau Coliseum, New York. The final shows were filmed and recorded for release in November as *Delicate Sound Of Thunder*.

The band toured again between May and July 1989. The red Strat remained David's main instrument for the A Momentary Lapse Of Reason/ Delicate Sound Of Thunder tours (1987-1989) and in June 1990 at Knebworth Park for the Nordoff-Robbins Music Charity show.

LA CARRERA PANAMERICANA

Hastily recorded at Olympic Studios, London in December 1991, David used both the cream Strat and the red Strat during sessions for the soundtrack to *La Carrera Panamericana* (a scenic film recreating the legendary seven day car race held in Mexico throughout the early 1950's). With an interest in motor racing, he took part in the event with Nick Mason and Steve O'Rourke (PF manager). Along with some excellent video footage captured by the film team, Pink Floyd's creative instrumentals contributed to the success of the project.

Right: David with Jon Carin (keyboards) at Olympic Studio,
London recording 'La Carrera Panamericana', December 1991
Below: David at the mixing desk with Andy Jackson

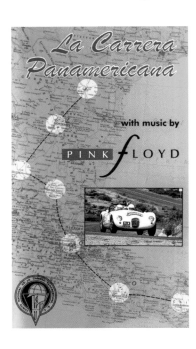

THE DIVISON BELL, 1994

In early 1993, Pink Floyd's album *The Division Bell* began with two weeks of playing and jamming in Britannia Row Studio, London, prior to recording at Astoria throughout the year. David's stunning guitar combined with the eloquently understated lyrics contributed to the success of the album. *Marooned* is possibly the most acclaimed Pink Floyd instrumental track, earning the band a Grammy in 1995. For both the recording sessions and during the following 1994 tour, he used the red Strat. Beginning in March, the tour spanned the US and Europe before culminating in three weeks of shows at London's Earls Court, some of which were filmed and recorded for release as *Pulse* .

The red Strat was David's guitar of choice for almost twenty years, until the return to favour of the Black Strat in 2005. Thereafter, it was used sparingly on his solo album, *On An Island*, and on the following tour in 2006.

8 BLACK IS BACK

It was now May 1997, the Black Strat had been on display in Hard Rock Café's for over ten years. If David was ever to use it again, it was time to request its return. When contacted, the Hard Rock Café were rather surprised to be asked to return the guitar. Claiming no knowledge of the existence of a loan agreement, they were under the assumption that they owned it. The original paperwork was produced to clear up any misunderstandings.

The Black Strat arrived back in England, sadly not in the same condition as when it left and without its original black case. For some inexplicable reason the Hard Rock Café, Miami, Florida had displayed the guitar unsecured and without a glass cabinet. It was hanging at eye level over a table, open to vandalism. This would account for its filthy, poor condition upon return with damaged and missing parts. To rectify the damage, the guitar went to Charlie Chandler's guitar workshop to be repaired.

The Black Strat (with parts missing) on display, The Hard Rock Café, Miami

DAVID GILMOUR MUSIC LIMITED

TEL: 44 (0) 81 83 165   FAX: 44 (0) 81 94706

Facsimile transmission

To fax no: 00 1 40 843 787   Company: Hardrock Cafe
Time: Date: 6 May 1997
No of pages: 1
Attention: Charlie Casella   From: Phil Taylor

Message

Re. David's Black Stratocaster serial no. 38797 - Hardrock Dallas

Please arrange to return the above mentioned guitar which has been on loan to you for the past 10 years, to me at the above address with its original case.

Please contact me if you have any problems or need any other information.

I have enclosed a copy of a letter for your information, confirming the agreement dated August 5th 1986.

Thank you for your help.

DAVID GILMOUR MUSIC LIMITED

TEL: 44 (0) 81 83 165   FAX: 44 (0) 81 94706

Facsimile transmission

To fax no: 00 1 40 843 787   Company: Hardrock Cafe
Time: Date: 7 June 1997
No of pages: 1
Attention: Charlie Casella   From: Phil Taylor

Message

Re. David's Black Stratocaster serial no. 38797 - Hardrock Dallas

Thank you for returning the above guitar I have just received it.
I am very disappointed to find the guitar in such a state. When I sent it to you it was in fine condition and when I have since seen it on display in Dallas it looked the same.
Apart from the guitar being in a filthy poor condition there are several missing parts.
These are:
Volume knob
Tone knob
pickup selector knob
tremolo arm and knob
The strap button at the end has been broken off leaving half a screw in the body and is missing.
Original case (it arrived with an ESP case)
Most of these parts must have been removed when it was taken off display.

Please look into this and let me know what you propose to do about it before I take the matter any further.

Thank you for your help.

Phil Taylor

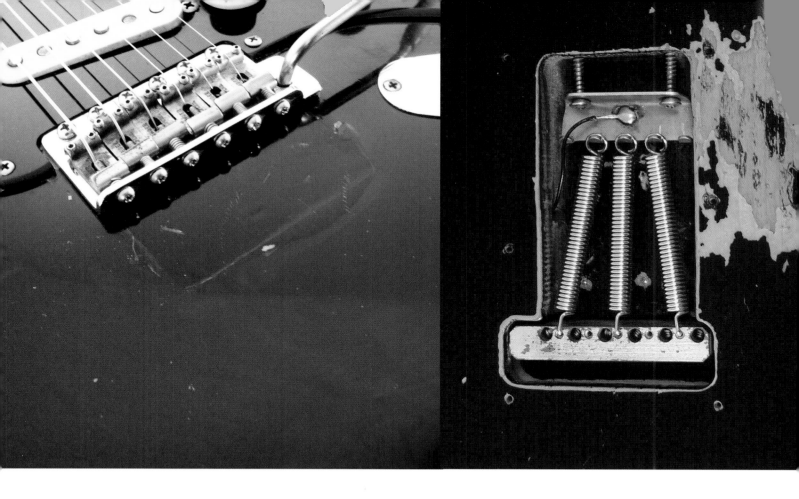

He was also asked to make some additional changes in order to restore it to being a good, playable instrument that David could use. The Kahler tremolo unit was removed, the hole filled with a suitable piece of wood and painted matching black. The preferred original Fender tremolo system was reinstalled and the Charvel neck with the locking nut was replaced with a new 57 vintage re-issue neck similar to the ones David was now using.

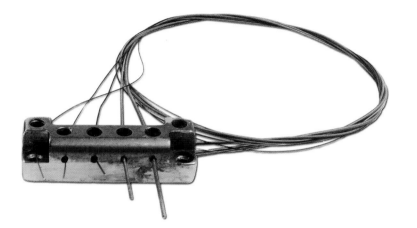

Top left: The original Fender tremolo bridge refitted, showing the repaired area of wood behind the bridge where the Khaler had been
Top right: Rear cavity showing original bridge now refitted with the tremolo spring arrangement and grounding wire
Above: Kahler tremolo bridge
Left: Kahler locking nut

Above: The original refitted Fender bridge

The original black case, silkscreened 'Pink Floyd London', has never been returned, The Hard Rock Café have been unable to locate it.

Although the Black Strat was back and ready to play, David rarely used it again until 2003.

THE DARK SIDE OF THE MOON
30TH ANNIVERSARY, 2003

To mark the 30th Anniversary of *The Dark Side Of The Moon* for their Classic Albums DVD series, Eagle Rock/Isis made a documentary about the writing, recording and making of this landmark album. Partially filmed at Astoria and Abbey Road Studios, London, David used the Black Strat to recreate some of the parts that he originally played on this guitar when the album was recorded in 1972/73.

The Dark Side Of The Moon has remained in the American Billboard charts for over 30 years, the longest duration in history.

"Perhaps the closest I will get to immortality will be through 'The Dark Side Of The Moon'. I think that record will go on being played for a while yet".

David Gilmour
SUNDAY TELEGRAPH 2006

123

THE INTERSTELLAR EXHIBITION, PARIS 2003/2004

In 2003, the Black Strat was displayed in the *Echoes* room at the Pink Floyd Interstellar Exhibition held at Cité de la Musique, Paris. Along with many other Pink Floyd historical items and memorabilia, it ran from 13th October to 15th January 2004.

The exhibition was considered a great success with the layout and artwork designed by Storm Thorgerson, a friend of David's since his Cambridge school days. It featured Storm's album covers with their iconic graphic images, along with his film and video footage which have embodied the music of Pink Floyd since 1968.

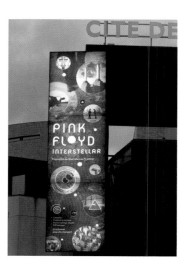

THE BLACK STRAT AT LIVE 8, 2005

The Black Strat's return to prominence was during the Pink Floyd rehearsals for Live8. The favoured red Strat had been used for the first two days of rehearsals at Black Island Studio, London. During the third day it was suggested that David should try the Black Strat, as he had used it on the original recordings of these songs. He put down the red one and began playing the Black Strat.

David's guitar sound instantly ascended to what can only be described as 'another level'. His body language changed, becoming animated and interacting with the guitar as if he had just discovered an old long-lost friend.

On stage at Live 8, Wembley, July 2005

Live 8 rehearsals,
Black Island Studio, London,
June 2005

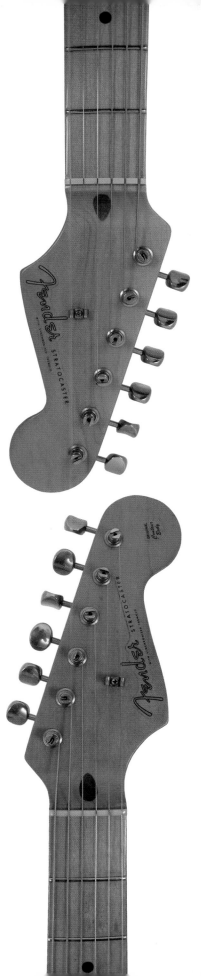

Right: Headstocks on the 57v reissue necks. The neck (1996-2005) – top picture from the Live8 reunion concert, is missing the 'Original Contour Body' mark. The one at the bottom fitted after Live8 is the earlier neck from 1983 taken off the 'About Face' tour cream Strat

On the 2nd July when David appeared on stage at Live8 in Hyde Park, London, it was an historic moment in the history of Pink Floyd. Live8 was a series of concurrent benefit concerts, timed to precede the G8 Summit (political conference of top world leaders), in support of the aims of the UK's 'Make Poverty History' campaign and the Global Call for Action Against Poverty. An estimated three billion people viewed the live broadcast. Not only was it the first time since The Wall shows at Earls Court, London, twenty four years previously that the band – David Gilmour, Richard Wright and Nick Mason had played together with Roger Waters – it was also over twenty years since David had last used the Black Strat in a live performance.

A NEW 57V NECK, 2005

After Live8, some of the frets on the Black Strat were slightly low and the neck required re-fretting. A change of fret wire was tried, but was unsuitable and David was due back in the studio to continue recording *On An Island*. As time was of the essence, the neck on the Black Strat was swapped with the neck from his 1983 57v cream Strat. It had been his main instrument for the 1984 About Face solo tour and David had only used it occasionally since. The cream Strat was used on stage with Pink Floyd at Live8 being played by Tim Renwick. The subtle differences in the shape of this neck felt more comfortable and better to play. Now with it's sixth neck, the Black Strat was firmly re-established as David's favourite Stratocaster guitar.

Facing page: Manufacture date visible on 57V neck
Above: Jose Moreno pictured in 2008 still making necks at the Fender Factory
in Corona, California, holding David's 57V neck which he made in 1983
Below: Name stamp on rear of neck

BLACK ON AN ISLAND, 2006

On An Island was recorded at Astoria, Abbey Road Studios and in David's home studio during 2005. With many of the lyrics written by Polly Samson, his wife, David commented, "She can express my thoughts better than I can. She thinks my guitar does my speaking for me, better than I can with words."

He produced the album, assisted by Phil Manzanera and Chris Thomas with orchestrations by Polish composer Zbigniew Preisner. Many distinguished musicians offered their contributions including Richard Wright, David Crosby and Graham Nash. He used a variety of different guitars for

Left: David's bithday party, Porchester Hall, London, March 2006, (left to right) Phil Manzanera, Steve DiStanislao, Guy Pratt and David
Below: Guy Pratt, Richard Wright, and David rehearsing for the 'On An Island' tour, Chiddingfold Club, February 2006

this project, including the Black Strat.

It was released to critical acclaim on 6th March 2006, a special date, David's birthday. He performed the new material for the first time at his party held at the Porchester Hall, London. An intimate and memorable evening with David playing new songs with his new band to a small audience of family and friends. Polly gave him a very special present for the occasion – a guitar strap previously owned by Jimi Hendrix. He used the strap on the Black Strat that night and throughout the tour.

Above: Awaiting soundcheck, Clam Castle, Austria, July 2006
Facing page: At the Royal Albert Hall, May 2006

His third solo album, *On An Island* is warm and lyrical with rich and emotive guitar work. It entered the UK chart at No.1 and was his first US Top 10 album as a solo artist.

Initial rehearsals for the On An Island tour took place at Chiddingfold Club, Surrey in February followed by production rehearsals at Black Island Studios, London. The tour was scheduled from March to May in special venues throughout Europe and the US, with added shows due to public demand in July and August. Locations included Radio City Music Hall, New York and St. Marks Square, Venice. The Black Strat featured prominently

Right: Still from 'Remember That Night', Royal Albert Hall
Below: Guy Pratt, Polly Samson and David, soundcheck, 'On An Island' tour 2006
Facing page: Soundcheck, Gdansk, Poland, August 2006

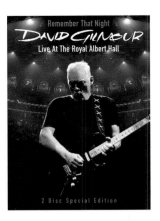

throughout the show, with David playing *On An Island* in its entirety as well as a selection of Pink Floyd classics. Three nights in May at the Royal Albert Hall, London were filmed in high definition by director David Mallet and released on DVD as *Remember That Night*.

For the final show of the tour in August, David performed in front of 50,000 people at the shipyards in Gdansk, Poland at the invitation of Solidarity and the mayor of Gdansk. For this very special occasion he was accompanied by the Symphony Orchestra of the Polish Baltic Philharmonic, conducted by Zbigniew Preisner. It was filmed, recorded and later released as *David Gilmour, Live In Gdansk*.

Recording the 'Live from Abbey Road' television show in Studio 1, Abbey Road, August 2006

9 BLACK HERE TODAY

The Black Strat is a 1969 black alder body with an original paint finish, chipped and worn through in places to reveal red and yellow paint underneath. The pickup cavity has additional routing. The wood infill behind the bridge is evident and the XLR hole repair visible on the body edge. With all of the changes and modifications, it remains David Gilmour's preferred Fender Stratocaster.

- Black pickguard was fitted in 1974, it has an additional recessed toggle switch for the neck pickup, fitted in 1978

- Tremolo arm is shortened to approximately 4.25"

- Neck and middle pickups are Fender from late 1971/early 1972, taken from the bullet neck Strat. The bridge pickup is a Seymour Duncan custom SSL-1 from 1978

- Volume pot is from the mid 1970's and the tone pots are dated 1971, taken from the bullet neck Strat

- Grounding has been rewired with additional copper shielding added

- Maple neck is a 1983 Fender 57V with Gotoh tuners

- Four-bolt neck plate is serial number 38979, fitted in 1972

- Bridge is the original from 1969, removed in 1983 and refitted in 1997

FENDER DAVID GILMOUR SIGNATURE MODEL

David had refused previous requests from Fender to copy his guitar, however, he was now assured that a definitive, high quality replica of his Black Stratocaster could be achieved at a cost that was affordable to both fans and guitar players.

In October 2006 Mike Eldred (head of Fender Custom Shop) and Todd Krause (Fender master builder) arrived in England to dissect, measure and take specific details in order to make a prototype replica of the Black Strat.

Several months later a specially adapted Stratocaster test guitar arrived with five pickguards, each fitted with sets of different pickups. These were changeable within seconds to enable pickup comparisons to be easily made.

In April 2007 the first prototype of the Black Strat arrived in England. Overall, it was found to be a good replication, requiring but a few changes. David compared his original Black Strat to the prototype and the different pickups in the test guitar to find the closest match.

Over the next few months, three further modified prototypes followed for approval. Before Fender would be allowed to begin production, the guitar had to meet David's high standards and be the best replica possible.

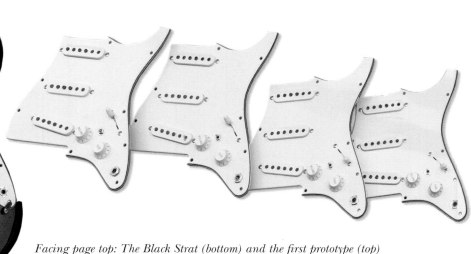

Facing page top: The Black Strat (bottom) and the first prototype (top)
Facing page right: Comparing body wear, knobs, pickguard material, body contours with first prototype

FINAL PROTOTYPES

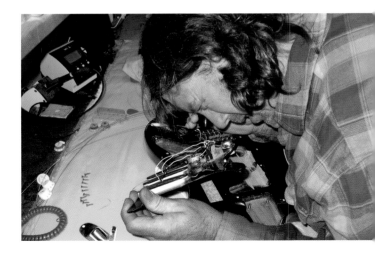

In March 2008 the Black Strat was taken to the Fender Custom Shop in Corona, California to spend three days with Master Builder Todd Krause. During this time every intricate detail of the guitar was checked and re-checked before the final prototype models were to be made.

Exact measurements were taken from the Black Strat. These included the profiles and contours of the neck and body, the pickguard material, the electronics and the appearance, look and feel of the aged, worn guitar. David wanted particular attention paid to replicating the sound of the pickups and their set-up along with the height and feel of the tremolo.

Two models have been produced. The first is a replica of the Black Strat as it is currently (showing signs of wear and tear). The second is a brand new replication of the Black Strat with the same parts and components (Fender refer to these as NOS), a 'new old stock' version of the guitar.

With the prototypes finally correct and acceptable, the project could now progress to the manufacturing phase. Two final prototypes of each model were made. One set are kept at the Fender Custom Shop as a reference from which all other David Gilmour Signature Stratocasters will be made. The other pair remains with David.

Top: Todd Krause inspecting the Black Strat
Centre: Prototype bodies
Right: Phil Taylor, the Black Strat, Todd Krause at the Fender Custom Shop
Facing page: Two of four final prototypes

10 ACCESSORIES TO BLACK

STRAPS

A selection of guitar straps used by David on the Black Strat since 1974.
Note: The brown Jimi Hendrix strap pictured on the left and a 1977
Schaefer Vega wireless transmitter first used for The Wall shows.

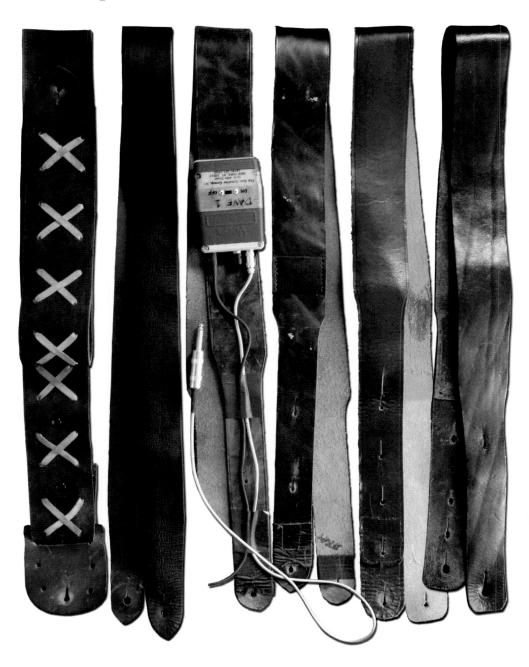

PICKS

Electric guitar picks used by David on the Black Strat (he uses different styles and weights for acoustic guitars). Shown in chronological order from top left: Plain Herco heavy - size 351 – used through the 1970's. In early 1980, during The Wall rehearsals in Los Angeles he changed to a smaller teardrop shape – size 354 – which he still uses, although Herco heavy 351's reappeared during the On An Island tour.

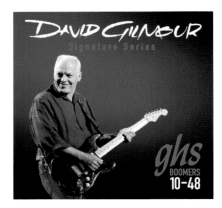

STRINGS

David originally used Gibson Sonomatic strings on the Black Strat. When Ernie Ball introduced the ability to purchase individual gauges in the early 1970's, he was able to choose the gauges that best suited him: 10, 12, 16, 28, 38, 48. David's gauges on Stratocasters have remained unchanged. Throughout the remainder of the 1970's he used Ernie Ball strings.

In 1979, while working on *The Wall* in Los Angeles, he purchased a guitar fitted with GHS Boomers, which he liked. He still uses Boomers and GHS have produced a custom David Gilmour set, available in his preferred gauges.

CASES

Over the years the Black Strat has travelled around the world in a number of different cases.

Left: Fender case: 1971 - stencil on left circa 'Pink Floyd: Live at Pompeii'
1977 - silkscreen on right circa 'Animals'
Below: Fender case: 1977 - silkscreen circa 'Animals'
Missing - not returned by The Hardrock Café

Left: Individual flight case: 1979 - silkscreen circa 'The Wall'

Above: Fender case: 1997 - current
Right: CP custom flight case with guitar drawers: 1987 - silkscreen Pink Floyd World Tour

OUTRO

Today, the Black Strat spends most of its time at David's home, ready to be called into action. It sometimes has a day out at his Astoria Studio or to his North London warehouse for a spot of maintenance or preparation for the occasional show, guest appearance or recording session.

In the end, it is just a guitar. When I sat down to write this book to accompany the proposed Fender replica model, David's reaction was that it was a daft idea… why write a book about an ordinary Strat that he bought nearly 40 years ago at Manny's?

It was a decent instrument back then. After all, David chose it. He has always been happy to make changes to it, and while some things haven't worked, others have. It has been well looked after, but never treated with much reverence. On one hand it is iconic, and on the other hand simply a Stratocaster, his working instrument, and that is how he has always viewed it.

That said, the Black Strat with its numerous changes is in itself a special guitar. If you have a rack full of the same model guitars and you pick them all up and play them, one will stand out. The Black Strat is like that. It just immediately feels comfortable. It has a great action, precise smooth tremolo and plays very nicely. It resonates well, and when plugged in sounds outstanding. The sound quality and playability set it apart. It is hard to quantify exactly what that special something is, but the Black Strat definitely has it.

A familiar special instrument in the hands of a great guitar player is where the magic lies. For them to be able to feel as one, in unison, with it enabling them to slip unhindered and uncompromised into the zone of creativity, with emotion, feel, touch, and dynamics for the music.

This is what I have been most privileged to witness and experience first hand over the years with David and the Black Strat.

Phil Taylor

ACKNOWLEDGEMENTS

My great thanks and appreciation to all who have helped and contributed, especially:

To the man himself - David Gilmour. Where does one start? My heartfelt thanks, both personally and professionally, for providing me with the opportunity and generally letting me do it my way for all of these years.

The ever-understanding love of my life - Cynthia, for her tremendous efforts, patience, encouragement, love and support.

To Langley Iddins, the designer of this book. A friend and a gentleman.

The irrepressible Storm Thorgerson, responsible for the cover design concepts and for being an absolutely unique force of nature and top-notch chap.

To Nick Mason for access to both his and Pink Floyd Management photo archives.

The fearsome twosome of Paul Loasby and Andy Murray at One Fifteen Management for services rendered.

Special thanks to: Vernon Fitch/Pink Floyd Archives - for his kind assistance with additional research and information; Paul Riordan; Jill Furmanovsky; Damon Iddins; Jessica Boudevin; Nadia Jones; Stephanie Roberts; Emile Lobo; Peter Barnes.

Phil Taylor with David Gilmour, Gdansk, August 2006

PHOTOGRAPHIC CREDITS

Amann/Dalle – 68, 80. Anna Wloch – 157, 160. Barry Plummer – 83, 85, 108. Bill Gavigan – 60. Brian Gibson – 86, 87. Brian Rasic – 135, 139. Courtesy of Capitol Records Photo Archive - 13. Charles Littledale – 1, 109. Chris Michie – 61. Classic Albums, Making of The Dark Side of The Moon – 29, 123. Claude Gassian – 26, 65. Clive Brooks – 117. Corbis/Preston – 101. Danièle Légeron – 38, 40. David Arroyo – 120. Edison vaz Melonio – 124. EMI Archive – 63. Fender Corp – 12, 16, 48, 146. Hilco Arendshorst – 9. Imageinphotography – 13, 17, 25, 29, 38, 45, 55. Jacques Bisceglia – 11. Jean Deni – 32. Jean Yves Legras – 81. Jill Furmanovsky/www. Rockarchive.com – 43, 51, 59, 62, 72, 75, 78, 79, 82, 84, 88, 101, 102, 104, 111, 119, 127, 128. John Baxter – 24. John Etchells – 94. Koh Hasebe/Shinko Music – 34, 47. Laurens van Houten – 30, 31. Langley Iddins – 4, 5, 15, 44, 57, 98, 106, 107, 110, 122, 142, 147, 149, 151. London Features Int. – 27, 49, 51, 59, 112. Mark Fisher – 103. Mark Grega – 134. Mike Prior – 97. Mirrorpix – 20, 119. Nick Mason Archive – 8, 9, 23, 35, 41, 53, 61, 69, 71, 95. Paul Riordan – 14, 17, 24, 46, 54, 57, 66, 67, 91, 108, 121, 148, 150, 151. Phil Taylor – 15, 56, 58, 76, 83, 91, 96, 99, 101, 107, 114, 116, 122, 129, 130, 131, 133, 136, 144, 145, 146, 151. Phillipe Gras – 26. Pink Floyd Archive – 10, 23, 36, 39, 73, 92. Pink Floyd Management – 12. Polly Samson – 137, 140, 141, 150, 154, 155. Redferns Music Picture Library – 28, 74, 88, 113, 118, 128. Redferns/Kirk – 70. Redferns/Verhorst – 110. Repfoto/Robert Ellis – 30, 31, 44, 46, 50, 52, 57, 58, 84, 90. Retna Pictures – 18, 115. Retna/McCabe – 152. Rex Features – 10, 37, 89, 126, 132. Rex/Everett – 40. Ritchie McHam – 114. Robin Constable – 54. Rupert Truman – front cover, 2, 3, 124, 125. Starfile – 71, 76. Storm Thorgerson – 6, 12. Universal Pictures – 29, 36, 37. Vernon Fitch – 54. Veuga/Dalle – 64. www.cyber-heritage.co.uk – 73, 74.

The author and publisher have made every reasonable effort to trace all copyright holders. Should there be any errors or ommissions please contact the publishers, we would be happy to correct them in future editions of the book.

ARTWORK AND DESIGN

Front cover, rear and title page images: Original concept by Storm Thorgerson and Dan Abbott at StormStudios, London

Location photographs on 'The Wave' at North Coyote Buttes, Paria Canyon/Vermillion Cliffs Wilderness, Arizona, USA
Art direction by Storm Thorgerson
Photography by Rupert Truman and Peter Curzon

Back cover: Hands, Design by Dan Abbott and Storm Thorgerson
Photography by Stuart Nichols

Book design and typography: Langley Iddins

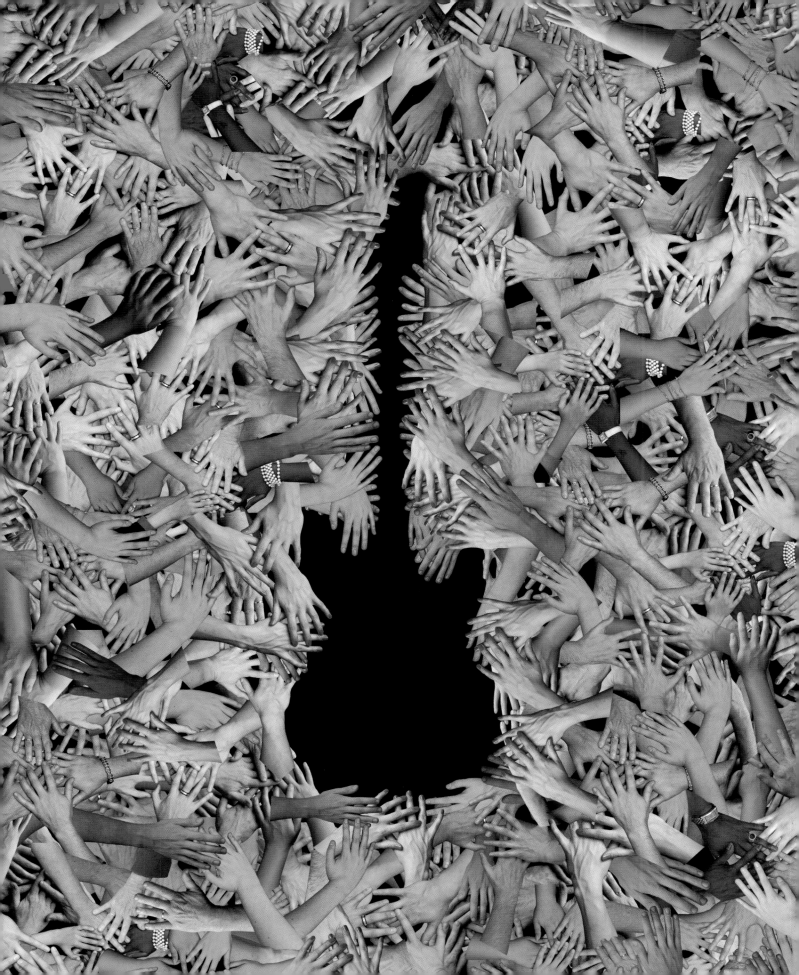

To be continued...